YOUR KNOWLEDGE HAS VALUE

Bibliographic information published by the German National Library:

The German National Library lists this publication in the National Bibliography; detailed bibliographic data are available on the Internet at http://dnb.dnb.de .

Imprint:

Copyright © 2017 GRIN Verlag
Print and binding: Books on Demand GmbH, Norderstedt Germany
ISBN: 9783668662711

This book at GRIN:

https://www.grin.com/document/416674

Dilan Prasad Harsha Senanayake

Comparative Analysis of the Social Life of Citizens and Political Interpretation Dublin, Chicago and Moscow

GRIN Verlag

GRIN - Your knowledge has value

Since its foundation in 1998, GRIN has specialized in publishing academic texts by students, college teachers and other academics as e-book and printed book. The website www.grin.com is an ideal platform for presenting term papers, final papers, scientific essays, dissertations and specialist books.

Comparative Analysis of the Social Life of Citizens and Political Interpretation of Three Different Cities: Dublin, Chicago and Moscow.

S. M. D. P. Harsha Senanayake

M.A. (Reading) International Relations, South Asian University, New Delhi, India.

B.A. (Hons.) International Relations, University of Colombo, Sri Lanka.

Diploma in International Political Economy, George Mason University, Virginia, USA.

Abstract

The paper discusses the political and social life of the citizens of Dublin, Chicago and Moscow based on three exceptional classics which written by three phenomenon authors in the world literature. The selected context describes the society in early World War period and how these respective cities changed due to external factors and variety of social forms. The changes which took place in respective cities directly influenced by the life and political behaviour of the people. Thus, the researcher analyzes the political and economic behaviour of the cities based on the concepts of "Voice, Loyalty and Exit."(Piketty, 2014)

The author describes the social context based on International Relations, the Hobbesian nature of the humans and illustrated the respective society. The entire paper is based on the original classics which were written by the respective authors and through that, the researcher attempted to provide a social review based on direct dimension. The research conducted to identify major social transformations and external, internal motives behind the social transformation. The role of the capital and the social classification identified as the major influence on the social reformation and the researcher exercised comparative analytical tools to draw a line among these three cities and common social behaviours of respective cities.

The role of religious institutions was a major social factor which influenced to the social life in these three different cities. Mainly the early war period made a dramatic changed of the capital and financial waves of the society and this dynamic role of the finance provided a background to the change of the social life. These two major reasons and five additional reasons bring to the conclusion by the author.

Key Words: Comparative analysis, Hobbesian Nature, Power, Religion, Social Classification

Content

1. Introduction

"Everything will turn out right, the world is built on that." (Bulgakov, 2011)

World literature performed a vital role to identify the global politics and world affairs. Mainly literature can be considered as one of the parameters to understand, analyze, and construct a political and social life of the humans and their social interactions. Through this paper, the researcher is attempting to identify the social phenomenon in early world war period based on three different novels which described three diverse cities. The first novel was "Dubliners" which written by James Joyce, the second novel was "Sister Carrie" authored by Theodore Dreiser and final book was "Master and Margarita" which written by Mikhail Bulgakov. Those novels described three cities: Dublin, Chicago and Moscow and those books given a complete picture of the life in those respective cities in term of politics, economic and social perspectives.

In this paper, the researcher mainly focuses on how these cities transformed its physical atmosphere, and how these physical and material changes constrained social life of the citizens based on political and social aspects. Mainly the researcher is attempting to do a comparative analysis based on these three novels and for that, the researcher uses the concept of "Voice, Exit, and Loyalty." Based on these three concepts the researcher is drawing a common parameter to analyze similarities and diversity of these three cities. The first session of the article is utilized by the author to give a brief idea about three novels which selected by the researcher to finalize this paper.

1.2. Three stories: short introduction and technical analysis.

The novel "Dubliners" was written by James Joyce in 1914 just before the World War I. It mainly focuses on the social and political changes which took place in the society due to domestic and international political, social changes. It's a collection of stories which address different dynamic factors and social faces.

Dublin city, society subjected to act of unions during the 1800s and they were able to abolish Ireland parliament. After that power struggles between British supporters and Irish independence movement shaped the city life up to 1922. (Joyce, 1914)

Mainly one year after the Dublin Lockout the tension started to escalate with the World War I. Nationalists in Dublin tied up the resistance moment and the Brish parliament found Dublin as a difficult opportunity for gain political advantages. The mixed responses over the United Kingdom have shaped the social structure of the Dubliners. In 1911 King George V entertained his visit in Dublin city with the gigantic support of the professional class of the Dublin. Majority of the professional class gained the political advantages with this visit of King George V. They gained the political prominence against the Protestant Ascendancy. The political power including the potentiality of control social dynamics shifted to emerging Catholic elites from the Protestants.

These power elites influenced to the city structure of Dublin city. the Grand Georgian houses on Mountjoy division, North Great George Street, Henrietta Street and many prosperous extents dominated by new elites. These avenues of the city provided homes to high-class professional including the Lawyers, Professionals, businessman then civil servants. This background note was a complete contrast to the rest of the citizens in Dublin. From the end of the 19th century, the wealth moved to suburbs and the dominant class refabricated the city with golf clubs, tennis clubs and modern transport mediums digest the city life.

The visible changes of the Dublin city demarcated the class division of the society. the less fashionable north side of the city provided shelter to thousands of the indigent citizens. The unskilled workers along with opportunity seekers shared these old buildings. Majority of the Dubliners stagnated into one roomed accommodations without any social recognition. The residents suffered appalling social conditions. The majority of the labours had to struggle with their life to survival.

The lack of major industrial hubs, finance and commerce droved the property of Dublin city. The presence of the foreign market in Dublin economy was able to slurp the wealth of Dubliners. The life of middle-lower class citizens became haunted due to these social factors.

The tragedy of Dublin city was portrayed by James Joyce through the Dubliners Nobel. The death of the city illustrated by Joyce and the book highlighted the powerless of the citizens. Joyce highlighted the political powerlessness of the citizens of Dublin. Many of the citizens paralyzed physically and mentally. Similarly, economic waves of the society including poverty motivated the citizens to behave in aberrant ways. All the stories in Dubliners illustrated the social life of the citizens through the lenses of realistic approach. However, the politics of language exercised by James Joyce depicts the skills of the author.

The writer used metaphorical and symbolic language to give a complete picture of Dublin city. According to the author if Dublin city disappeared from the world map, "Dubliners" will provide an idea about the Dublin city and the life of Dublin. The story based on characters of Old Collier, Father Flynn, Molly Bloom, Mohany and few other main characters. Based on these individual stories, the author tried to portrait a realistic picture of the Dublin and social changes of the city. The book described the Hobbesian nature of the humans and most of the stories focused on simony, truancy, pederasty, Child abuses, spouse abuses, gambling, and nasty brutal behaviour of humans. James Joyce used the concept of paralyzing, corruption and dead to link these individual behaviours with the city.

The story of Sister Carrie was a great piece written by Theodore Dreiser in 1900. The story based on the life of Sister Carrie. The author described the character as a courageous, honest, intelligence and unselfishness character. But the researcher has a different argument about the characteristics of Sister Carrie. The story portrays the political and social changes which took place in Chicago city. Mainly, with the American industrial revolution, Chicago city subjected to colossal changes in terms of industrial zones and other larger factories.

Industrial revolution clearly demarcated the social classification; further, it formulated physical polarization as well. City divided into many layers and Sister Carrie is giving a vibrant image of the socio, political and economic life of Chicago during 1900s. With the industrial revolution, the social capital placed on a minority of the society. This wealthy class started to dominate the city life with the colossal access to the social opportunities. The prosperity and richness of the city were occupied by the profit makers. New housing programs initiated with the influence of the upper-class families. Clubs, Branded clothing and dining outlets, polo and golf grouds coloured the residential areas of the upper class. The rapid development of industrialization changed the social life of the citizens. Mainly, the polarization of the labour forces including attitudes of profit maximizations created an eight hours labour services.

The unskilled labour flows to Chicago city from all around the world. Many of the unskilled labours from Eastern and Southern Europe, including Poles, Lithuanians, Ukrainians,

Hungarians, Czechs, Slovaks, Greeks, and Italians flows to Chicago and settled in the west side of the city. The amateurish white labours including characters like sister Carrie drifted to Chicago and most of these white labour forces settled in suburban areas and south side of the city accommodated the black labour force. With the support of the wealthier class of the society, Northern and Western part of the city started to developed. Many reputed schools and other public resources developed in this areas while other parts of the city remained backwards. The city structure of Chicago during 1990s portrayed the de facto segregation of the society. The industrial realities disturbed by the war ways in the city and many of the river systems including Chicago river, Lake Michigan. Sister Carrie first time visited Chicago to flourish her life in terms of economic prosperity.

She entered to train with rural and middle-class identification and during this journey she met Charlie Drouet. He was a good looking decent person. Once Sister Carrie settles down with her sister, Carrie was entered into Chicago labour force. One day she lost her job and she ended her life with Charlie Drouet. After that Sister Carrie's life subject to many differences. She seduced by Charlie and George Hurstwood; another character of the Novel disintegrated her life as he was exercising his money, attractive appearance, and romantic verbal communication skills to get Sister Carrie's attention. However, he intentionally concealed his marital status. Ms Hurstwood realized this unethical affiliation between her husband and Sister Carrie and she got the divorce from her husband. Then Sister Carrie and Hurstwood left the city. (Cliff notes, Sister Carrie)

Chicago city sunk into social stress. Human behaviour shaped by incompleteness and the competition. Mainly industrialization process changed the human behaviour and complement with materialist life. Thus moral values and role of religion fed off from the social structure. Again "Voice, Exit and Loyalty" shaped the socio, political and economic face of Chicago society. Similar to James Joyce, Theodore Dreiser, correspondingly highlighted the Hobbesian nature of human behaviour, deviant acts of society, social classification and separation between religion and society due to industrialization. Mainly author was able to highlight "industrial- mechanistic reality" of the society.

Mikhail Bulgakov rendered the socialist reality in the Communist Soviet Union based on Moscow city. "Master and Margarita" is the perfect picture to understand socialist reality.

The power accumulation of Stalin over communist Russia succeeded in the 1920s. It was eventually noticeable the end of the liberalization of the society and economy of Russia. All the dynamics features of the social process subjected to government control. The terrorization of society in Russia and other republics of the USSR legitimated under the Stalin power. The centralization of the wealth and economic process influenced to the social order and well-being of the citizens of Russia. Agriculture and industries endured by the brutal force of centralizations under the Stalin regime. The cultural freedom restructured by the Stalin power and it negatively impacted to the social stability. Thousands of individuals were eliminated by the brutality of Stalin government. These actions cultivated fear and hazard over the society. The communist party governed the social wealth and it influenced to the life and prosperity of the labour forces in Russia.

A wide range of regimentation replaced the social order as a result of collective industrialization. Collective enterprises substituted individualistic efforts across the country including Moscow. The new agenda of Stalin government inactivated the development of the society and great terror of the government bought the Satan to the Russian society. Mikhail Bulgakov cleverly addressed these social transformations and the dynamic waves of the social life of the citizens through Master and Margarita.

The Book is written in between 1928 and 1940 but Published in 1967. The story simply describes how Satan or the devil entered into Soviet society. (Belyk, The Master and Margarita)

Master, Margarita, Woland and Yeshua and several characters used to present these social realities to the reader. Imperialist Russia governed by Nicolas II and 1917 revolution was able to draught political, socio and economic change in Russian society. Whole society upgraded to the collective labour force. Impulsive economic and industrial development flourished the Soviet society. Moscow identified as a pivotal point of this industrial process and many counter-revolutions deter the social stability. Nationalist ideology reshaped by communist identity. The author describes these physical, ideological and epistemological changes based on Moscow city. Corruption, political crimes, prostitution and bolshie behaviour of Moscow society identified as a devil by the author. This identification is mostly similar to Hobbesian nature of human behaviour. Thus the researcher utilizes "Hobbesian Nature of Human Behavior" as one parameter to compare these three books and respective cities.

1.3. Religion and the society

James Joyce highlighted the religious crisis of the Dublin society. Protestants and British church involved with continuous power struggle since the 1800s'. Because of that Dublin society stagnated and no social modification placed in Dublin. He describes this situation metaphorically by using a term of "Paralyze."(Cliff Notes, About Dubliners)

Most of the religious institutions were corrupted and religious leaders subjected to financial frauds. Especially Character of Father Flynn was a symbolic presentation of the Roman Catholic Church. In a very first story, Joyce describes how Father Flynn paralyzed and given information about his death. Irish political and social institutions were frozen between Roman Catholic society and British church, and it deters the social development and moral development of the society. Contradictions of religion placed social unrest and particularly within the youth. People discriminate other religious believers. Mainly in the second story "An Encounter" of the book he mentioned,

"A spirit of unruliness diffused itself among us and, under its influence, differences of culture and constitution were waived. We banded ourselves together, some boldly, some in jest and some almost in fear: and of the number of this latter...." (Joyce, 1914)

Social unrest and religion polarization of the society completely stagnated the social development and establish abhorrence among the youth.

"...the ragged troop screaming after us: 'Swaddlers! Swaddlers!' thinking that we were Protestants because of Mahony, who was dark- complexioned, wore the silver badge of a cricket club in his cap." (Joyce, 1914)

Expressly, Roman Catholic Church associates with corruptions in many ways; it changed the entire social moralities and spiritual life of Dubliners. Many of the stories of Dubliners described the Hobbesian nature of the citizens of Dublin. They used to have alcohol, citizens spent their money to prostitution, because religious institutions corrupted and those institutions are not pure enough to address or to develop social moralities. Because of this simony, truancy, pederasty and drunkenness; moral and spiritual aspects of the society sunk in the darkness. No economic boom took place in the society.

Dublin City does not have any social or moral progress, wealth or any development and its paralyzed forever, but a death of Father Flynn gave new hope to the citizen. This death can be identified as a metaphorical death.

"...the selling to its members by the Roman Catholic Church of blessings pardons or other behaviours..."(Dreiser, 1981)

Religion polarization paralyzed the Dublin and this situation morsel to Chicago city as well. Mainly when it comes to "Sister Carrie" she identified herself as a religious character. But social movements and industrialization process of Chicago city totally change her moral aspects. While she is travelling the train to Chicago she describes the physical changes which she victimized.

"She gazed at the green landscape now passing it swift review until her swifter thoughts replaced its impression with vague conjectures of what Chicago might be." (Dreiser, 1981)

But once she entered the city she describes the city based on material values and physical appearance of the city.

"The city full of thousands of cars and a clangour of engine bells. Heavy traffics decorated the city with smoky mills. Chicago River was too little muddy creek, crowed with the huge masted wanderers from far-off waters nosing the black, posted banks." (Dreiser, 1981)

These physical conditions showcased the materialistic reality of the city. Industrialization was defilement the moral aspects of the citizens of Chicago.

"...the city its cunning wiles no less than the infinitely smaller and more human temper." (Dreiser, 1981). When it comes to Dubliners and Master and Margarita, those books did not give any direct visualization of the city structures; however, Sister Carrie was able to portrait clear picture of the city structure.

With the industrialization, moral aspects of the human behaviour erased from their social life and that space replaced by the incompleteness and the competition. People detached from the religion. Their spiritual life involved with the mechanical life. Most of the middle-class family

10

members started their labour life early in the morning and end it in the late evening. During the daytime, they are continuously struggling with machines and ultimately they became victims of the profit base market system. No human feelings deal with their life and industrial reality was cultivated brutality and necessity of using cohesive arbitrary power towards weak persons of hierarchical order. The system did not create any space for moral values and a whole system governed by the fittest persons based on their own will. According to the author, the entire society turned into goal seeking society and individual aspirations highlighted rather than common communal values. Mainly Chicago city and the people in Chicago detach from the church. They try to establish a secure social system with capitalism.

Due to these circumstances and fewer affiliations with religion entities youth enjoyed their life freely. Most of the times, their lives were vulnerable to social threats and less respect for humanity. For instance, Sister Carrie failed to report her work due to her bad physical conditions since she was exposed to wicked winter in Chicago. She got the notice from the industrial zone which she used to work mentioning that "she got fired." We can analyze this incident based on moral aspects and the industrial reality. According to moral aspects, the company owners can consider her inability and physical conditions. But they did not want to consider about their employee due to industrial realities. No matter what was happened to their employee's; ownership only considers their profit and their market values. Even when it comes to Sister Carrie's life in her worked place, she had to face immoral working environment. No mental or physical freedom offered to workers by the management.

Dubliners did not portrait any image of the seductions which took place in society. But when it comes to Sister Carrie main two characters of the book intentionally seduced Carrie. Particularity, a character of Hurstwood concedes his material status and enthralled Sister Carrie by using his financial and economic power. We can analyze this situation based on religious institutions. Since the presence of the religious institutions and their influence on the society is more powerful, it can deter the deviant behaviours of the social life.

"Even at night, in the moonlight, I have no rest... Why did they trouble me? Oh, gods, gods..." (Bulgakov, 2011)

If we compared Master and Margarita in this context we can identify clear differences on the religious institutions of Soviet Russia. Russians continuously detached from the religious

11

institutions under the Nicolas II administration and the communist regime, Communist regime prioritizes communist and Marxist ideas in their society. The different between Chicago and Moscow was, industrialization process in Chicago mobilize the idea "individualism." Moscow under the communist regime highlighted the spirit of common life. But all the three societies suck in many deviant social phenomena. For instance drugs, alcohol, corruption, and social unrest. Industrialization and presence of communism completely change the city structure and bureaucratic hierarchy of the Soviet Union. Soviet revolution and counter-revolutions which placed in Soviet society were able to mobilize social unrest. Many of the liberal thinkers and revisionist left the country. Money, War, conflicts, and weapons became a necessary factor in the Russian society. These factors completely destroyed the moral and spiritual life of the Moscow citizen. The book itself highlighted the deviant behaviour of the citizens. Most of the Russians highly addicted to alcohol including vodka.

Master and Margarita bought the idea of Satan-devil into the picture. Under the communist regime, they stared the common labour forces. Those labour forces directed to agriculture and economic development process. Thus, Moscow city subjected to colossal economic boom. However, quality of life and prosperity of individuals decreased gradually. Because of that person committed social crimes. Moscow became a concourse to social crimes and people rid away from moral life because they wanted to survive somehow within the society. Religion institutions subjected to the power of communist party and most of the religious institutions corrupted by itself.

These three books were given a deep understanding of the religious institutions and the connections they had with the respective societies. Based on these facts we can analyze that before the world war period region and the society maintain respective breach between each other due political, socio and economic changes. Mainly industrialization and religious conflicts highlighted and strengthen this segregation.

1.4. "Voice, Exit and Loyalty"

"No one's fate is of any interest to you except your own." (Belyk, The Master and Margarita)

With the socialist revolution, most of the people left the country and people who were not capable enough to leave the country were stagnate under the communist administration. Communist leadership redirected the labour focuses on the common labour market. These people were not able to transfer their voices to administrative level. Most of the people framed into communist ideology and their exit ability blocked by the government. The rule of the communist party established a social hierarchical order and the communist party members placed themselves top on the ladder. The author primarily focused on the communist face under the Stalin regime. The government appointed their party members to monitor the civil activities of the society. Industrial zones, villages, common labour villages monitored by these special secret services. According to the author, the messengers of devil lives among the citizens and labours. Thus, the citizens restricted themselves and their voice. The people had no alternatives to pick up except believing the Stalin government. The people's voice did not reflect by the communist regime and the people who had the ability to shift their loyalty left the Russian homeland during the revolution and early days of the communist regime.

"But what is most terrifying is not the executioner, but the unnatural light in the dream, coming from a cloud that is boiling and tumbling on the earth, as always at moments of world catastrophe." (Bulgakov, 2011)

The metaphors and symbolic language of the writer emphasize the social realities and this technique used by the author through the Master and Margarita to fastener the readers. Under the Stalin regime, many of the Soviet citizens had to bequeath their heads to the guillotine. Freedom of the people was condemned by the Stalin government. The power of voice and liberty de-attached from the citizen. The changes of the weather depict the social transformation which took place in the communist Russia. The light and prosperity devoured by the satan.

This situation was absolutely analogous to Chicago and Dublin. When it comes to Chicago, the government did not represent the voices of a middle class and middle-class families dedicated entire life inside the industrial zones. Even in Dublin people who had capabilities, they took the "exit" opportunities and people who have fewer abilities were struck in the political wetlands.

"You want to see Lincoln Park, he said, and Michigan Avenue. They are putting up great buildings there. It's a second New York, great. So much to see-theatres, crowds, fine houses-oh you'll like that." (Dreiser, 1981)

Chicago city builds up with the clear division of the city structure and people who capable enough to represent their voices in a political system used to live in the luxurious part of the city. The clear partition of the city and its infrastructure facilities demarcated the social life of the citizens. Mainly, the prosperous area of the city developed according to the will of the rich person and the people who control the economy. The desires of the upper-class societies reflected through the city structure. New cinema theatres, Café and coffee shops, branded textile and dress factories and luxurious apartments establish in the city to address the upper-class social requirements. But the industrialization or the political flow of Chicago city did not address the requirements of the middle-class families and the people who migrate to Chicago city to as a labour face. Many of them settled in near the Chicago River and with the minimum quality of life. The lumpy neighbourhood and the less capability to mobilize their economic standard deter the voice of these middle class and migrated peoples.

When it comes to Minnie's family they struggled to pay their house rent and they had a minimum quality of life. As they belonged to middle-class labour society. Thus, they didn't have any potentiality to exit from current social states. Their loyalty strictly relayed on the government and the capitalist system. Money placed the vital role in social structure and market system and it was the key to enter into social opportunities. The people who control the financial system enjoyed their in a magnified way and relished the social infrastructures. However, the middle-class families spent their entire life in the factories and sunk in the darker side of the industrial reality.

"Dubliners" also describe the concept of "voice exit and loyalty." (Piketty, 2014) The natural face of the city completely changed due to social modifications and due to religious activities, corruption paralyzed society. Most of the people left the country and settled somewhere in Europe.

"...onetime they used to be a field there in which they used to play every evening with other people's children. Then a man from Belfast bought the field and build houses in it" (Dreiser, 1981)

Most of the children and citizens left the country or else they settle down in better places in the country. Dublin city deep into economic and political crisis, poverty, corruption, and city subjected to political movements against British imperialism.

"...this channel of poverty and inaction the Continent sped its wealth and industry." (Joyce, 1914)

Dubliners demarcated the ideology of the people who exit from the Dublin and gave their loyalty to another sovereignty state. The people who exist from the society identify the Dublin as a dirty and poor place. In that sense, the author highlighted the quality of the life of the people who lived in the Dublin city. They had to struggle with the economy to survive and see the lights of future. Their loyalty vested in the government and they had to believe that the government will able to colour their life. Therefore, they relayed on the government and the same time the lack of exit capabilities forced them to rely on the government. Those people had to stay with the city like the enginemen's of the sinking ship.

2. Conclusion

The stories were colossal inside revive of the three different cities and mainly those books portraits how the city structure and political waves of the society influenced to the life of the people and vice versa. The political life of the society inherently affiliated with the economic face of the society. Thus, the people who control the financial statues were able to print their voice on the political agenda of the city. Same time the governments and the policy makers relayed on the upper class of the social ladder in terms benefits they received from the economic class. These vice versa conditions deter the voice of middle class and other classes of the social order. Thus, the middle class and the people who did not control the money flow had to retain on the government. The three different cities addressed the three different social problems and circumstances: religious conflicts, social stagnations, industrial realities, and the communist reality. However, all the books highlighted the role of the economy and the power of the finance; since it was the major requirement to bring the voice of the people to policymakers. Similarly, it shaped the citizens choice of exit and loyalty.

These details provided sufficient reading about the role social classification. How it placed on the respective cities, economies and political life of citizens of these cities.

These three books demarcating the social realities of respective cities based on particular time period. Role of the economy decided the social life in everywhere and because of that natural behaviour of humans motivated them to earn money to enter to the better social cluster. Thus people kill their moralities, moral values and engaged with the unstoppable struggle to take the hegemony over the fellow citizens.

References

About Dubliners. (n.d). Retrieved January 2, 2018, from Cliff notes, Houghton Mifflin Harcourts Website, https://www.cliffsnotes.com/literature/d/dubliners/about-dubliners

Belyk, Kristina. (n.d.). The Master and Margarita: Deconstructing Social Realism. Retrieved December 27, 2017, from Brighton online, Brighton UK Website, http://arts.brighton.ac.uk/study/literature/brightonline/issue-number-three/the-master-and-margarita-deconstructing-social-realism

Bulgakov, Mikhail. (2011). Master and Margarita. Landon: Penguin Books Ltd.

Cliff Notes Sister Carrie. (n.d.) Retrieved December 25, 2017, from Cliff notes, Houghton Mifflin Harcourts, https://www.cliffsnotes.com/literature/s/sister-carrie/critical-essays/symbolism-in-sister-carrie

Dreiser, Theodore. (1981). Sister Carrie- The Pennsylvania Edition. Pennsylvania: University of Pennsylvania Press.

Joyce, James. (1914). Dubliners. New York, NY: Oxford University Press.

Piketty, Thomas. (2014). Capital in the 21st Century. New York, NY: Harvard University Press.